Unveiling the USA Patriot Act: Analyzing Its Impact on Civil Liberties

AF437148

Copyright Page

TITLE: Unveiling the USA Patriot Act: Analyzing Its Impact on Civil Liberties

1ST Edition

Copyright @ 2023

Roberto M. Rodriguez. All rights reserved.

ISBN: 9798215437032

Table of Contents

Unveiling the USA Patriot Act: Analyzing Its Impact on Civil Liberties

By Roberto Miguel Rodriguez

Introduction to the USA PATRIOT Act

- Overview of the USA PATRIOT Act and its historical context

- Explanation of the purpose and objectives of the Act

- Introduction to the different sections and provisions of the Act

Historical Background of Civil Liberties in the United States

- Examination of the historical development and significance of civil liberties in the United States

- Discussion of landmark court cases and legislation that have shaped civil liberties in the country

- Analysis of the balance between national security and civil liberties prior to the enactment of the USA PATRIOT Act

The USA PATRIOT Act: Key Provisions and Controversies

- Detailed explanation of the key provisions of the Act, including surveillance, intelligence gathering, and law enforcement powers

- Examination of the controversies surrounding the Act, including concerns over privacy invasion and potential abuse of power

- Analysis of the legal and constitutional implications of the Act's provisions

Impact on Individual Rights and Privacy

- Assessment of the impact of the USA PATRIOT Act on individual rights and privacy

- Discussion of specific cases and examples highlighting the infringement on civil liberties

- Examination of the effectiveness of the Act in achieving its intended goals

Legal Challenges and Court Rulings

- Overview of the legal challenges brought against the USA PATRIOT Act

- Analysis of significant court rulings and their implications for civil liberties

- Evaluation of the role of the judiciary in safeguarding individual rights in the context of national security

Public Opinion and Debates Surrounding the Act

- Exploration of public opinion on the USA PATRIOT Act and its impact on civil liberties

- Analysis of the debates and discussions surrounding the Act, including arguments for and against its provisions

- Examination of the role of media, advocacy groups, and public discourse in shaping public opinion

Policy Recommendations and Future Implications

- Proposal of policy recommendations to address the concerns raised by the USA PATRIOT Act

- Evaluation of potential changes to the Act or alternative approaches to balancing national security and civil liberties

- Discussion of the potential future implications of the Act on individual rights and privacy in the United States

Conclusion: The Legacy of the USA PATRIOT Act

- Recapitulation of the main findings and arguments presented throughout the book

- Assessment of the long-term impact of the Act on civil liberties in the United States

- Final thoughts on the importance of vigilance and proactive measures to protect individual rights and privacy in the face of national security challenges.

Chapter 1: Introduction

Background of the USA PATRIOT Act

The USA PATRIOT (Uniting and Strengthening America by Providing Appropriate Tools Required to Intercept and Obstruct Terrorism) Act was signed into law by President George W. Bush on October 26, 2001, in response to the devastating terrorist attacks that occurred on September 11, 2001. This landmark legislation aimed to enhance the ability of law enforcement agencies to prevent and investigate acts of terrorism within the United States.

The 9/11 attacks exposed several shortcomings in the nation's intelligence and law enforcement capabilities, as well as loopholes in existing laws that hindered their ability to detect and prevent future terrorist activities. The USA PATRIOT Act was enacted to address these deficiencies and provide authorities with the necessary tools to combat terrorism effectively.

The Act expanded the powers of law enforcement agencies, particularly the FBI and the intelligence community, by granting them greater authority to share information, conduct surveillance, and collect intelligence on potential terrorist threats. It also facilitated cooperation and information sharing between law enforcement agencies at the federal, state, and local levels, as well as with foreign governments.

Critics argue that the USA PATRIOT Act has had a significant impact on civil liberties and individual rights, particularly regarding privacy. The Act granted law enforcement agencies the authority to conduct surveillance and collect information on individuals suspected of involvement in terrorism, even without probable cause. This has raised concerns about the potential for abuse and violations of privacy rights.

Furthermore, the Act expanded the scope of the Foreign Intelligence Surveillance Act (FISA), allowing for the surveillance of individuals not necessarily associated with foreign terrorist organizations. Critics argue that this expansion has blurred the lines between intelligence gathering and criminal investigations, potentially leading to the unwarranted surveillance of innocent individuals.

The USA PATRIOT Act also broadened the definition of "domestic terrorism," which some argue could be used to target political activists and dissenters, infringing on their rights to free speech and association.

In conclusion, the USA PATRIOT Act was enacted as a response to the 9/11 attacks, with the aim of enhancing national security and preventing future acts of terrorism. However, its impact on civil liberties and individual rights, particularly in terms of privacy, has been a subject of debate. It is essential to analyze the effects of this legislation critically and strike a delicate balance between national security and the protection of individual freedoms.

Purpose and scope of the book

The book titled "Unveiling the USA PATRIOT Act: Analyzing its Impact on Civil Liberties" serves as a comprehensive examination of the effects of the USA PATRIOT Act on individual rights and privacy. Aimed at a wide audience consisting of undergraduate and graduate students, high school students, academics and researchers, policy makers and government officials, journalists, business professionals, military and defense personnel, think tanks and analysts, the general public, librarians and educators, non-government organizations, diplomats and international workers, as well as book clubs, this subchapter provides an overview of the book's purpose and scope.

The purpose of this book is to critically analyze the USA PATRIOT Act, a landmark legislation enacted in response to the 9/11 terrorist attacks, and its impact on civil liberties. It seeks to shed light on the various provisions of the Act and how they have affected individual rights and privacy within the United States. Through a balanced and evidence-based approach, the book aims to inform readers about the potential consequences of such legislation on democratic societies.

The scope of this book is broad, covering a wide range of topics related to the USA PATRIOT Act and its implications for civil liberties. It delves into the historical context that led to the Act's enactment, exploring the political climate, public sentiment, and security concerns prevalent at the time. Furthermore, the book examines the specific provisions of the Act, such as surveillance measures, information sharing between government agencies, and expanded powers of law enforcement, and assesses their impact on individual privacy and rights.

Additionally, the book analyzes the legal challenges and court rulings that have shaped the interpretation and application of the USA PATRIOT Act. It explores the ongoing debates surrounding the Act's effectiveness in combating terrorism versus its potential infringement on civil liberties. The book also highlights the perspectives of various stakeholders, including privacy advocates, government officials, legal experts, and affected individuals, providing a comprehensive and balanced view of the Act's consequences.

Through its comprehensive analysis, the book aims to stimulate critical thinking and informed discourse among its diverse audience. It seeks to empower readers with the knowledge and understanding necessary to engage in meaningful conversations about the delicate balance between national security and civil liberties. Ultimately, this book aims to contribute to a more informed and nuanced understanding of the USA PATRIOT Act and its impact on individual rights and privacy.

Importance of analyzing the impact on civil liberties

Examining the effects of the USA PATRIOT Act on individual rights and privacy is of utmost importance in today's society. This subchapter titled "Importance of Analyzing the Impact on Civil Liberties" sheds light on the significance of understanding the implications of this legislation for a wide range of audiences, including undergraduate and graduate students, high school students, academics and researchers, policy makers and government officials, journalists, business professionals, military and defense personnel, think tanks and analysts, the general public, librarians and educators, non-government organizations, diplomats and international workers, and book clubs.

For undergraduate and graduate students, this subchapter provides an opportunity to critically analyze the USA PATRIOT Act's impact on civil liberties, fostering a deep understanding of the balance between national security and individual rights. By exploring case studies and legal precedents, students can develop a comprehensive perspective on the Act's implications, equipping them to engage in informed discussions and contribute to the ongoing discourse surrounding civil liberties.

High school students, as future citizens and potential leaders, need to be aware of the trade-offs between security and privacy. By studying the USA PATRIOT Act's impact on civil liberties, they can develop a nuanced understanding of the legislation's consequences and become active participants in shaping public policy.

Academics and researchers play a crucial role in analyzing the USA PATRIOT Act's impact on civil liberties. By examining empirical evidence and conducting studies, they can provide valuable insights into the Act's long-term effects on individual rights and privacy. Their research can inform policy debates, drive legislative reforms, and contribute to the protection of civil liberties.

Policy makers and government officials have a responsibility to understand the implications of the legislation they enact. This subchapter equips them with a comprehensive overview of the USA PATRIOT Act's impact on civil liberties, allowing them to make informed decisions that strike an appropriate balance between security and individual rights.

For journalists, business professionals, and the general public, this subchapter serves as a reliable source of information on the USA PATRIOT Act's impact on civil liberties. In an era marked by increasing threats to privacy, understanding the consequences of this legislation is essential for safeguarding individual rights.

Librarians, educators, and book clubs can utilize this subchapter to promote critical thinking and engage their communities in discussions about civil liberties. By delving into the analysis of the USA PATRIOT Act's impact, they can foster a deeper understanding and appreciation of the importance of protecting individual rights.

Non-government organizations, diplomats, and international workers can draw valuable insights from this subchapter to advocate for the protection of civil liberties both domestically and internationally. By understanding the impact of the USA PATRIOT Act, they can contribute to the development of policies that safeguard individual rights while addressing security concerns.

In conclusion, analyzing the impact of the USA PATRIOT Act on civil liberties is vital for various audiences. By providing nuanced insights into the effects of this legislation, this subchapter aims to foster a deeper understanding of the balance between security and individual rights.

Chapter 2: Understanding Civil Liberties

Definition and significance of civil liberties

Civil liberties are fundamental rights and freedoms that are guaranteed to individuals by a government and protected by the law. They are essential for the functioning of a democratic society and are designed to safeguard individual autonomy, privacy, and personal dignity. Civil liberties include but are not limited to freedom of speech, assembly, religion, and the press, as well as the right to privacy, due process, and equal protection under the law.

The significance of civil liberties lies in their role in preserving the balance between the power of the government and the rights of individuals. They serve as a check on the potential abuse of authority by those in positions of power. Civil liberties are a crucial aspect of the social contract between citizens and their government, ensuring that individuals are protected from unjust actions and that their basic human rights are respected.

In the context of the USA PATRIOT Act, understanding the definition and significance of civil liberties is paramount. The Act, passed in response to the 9/11 terrorist attacks, granted the government enhanced surveillance and investigative powers, raising concerns about potential encroachments on civil liberties.

Examining the impact of the USA PATRIOT Act on civil liberties is of utmost importance for various stakeholders. For undergraduate and graduate students, high school students, academics, and researchers, understanding this impact is crucial for studying and analyzing the implications of counterterrorism measures on individual rights and privacy.

Policy makers and government officials need to be aware of the potential consequences of legislation on civil liberties to strike a balance between national security and protecting individual freedoms. Journalists and the general public benefit from understanding the impact of the Act to hold the government accountable and engage in informed discussions on civil liberties.

Business professionals, military and defense personnel, think tanks, and analysts should be aware of the implications of the Act for their respective areas of interest, as it may affect their operations, ethical considerations, and assessments of national security policies.

Librarians, educators, and non-government organizations play a vital role in educating the public about civil liberties, privacy rights, and the implications of the USA PATRIOT Act. They can provide resources, organize discussions, and raise awareness about the importance of protecting civil liberties in a democratic society.

Diplomats, international workers, and book clubs can benefit from understanding the impact of the Act to engage in cross-cultural dialogues on human rights, privacy, and national security.

By examining the effects of the USA PATRIOT Act on civil liberties, individuals from various backgrounds and niches can contribute to a well-informed and balanced discussion on the delicate balance between national security and protecting individual rights and privacy.

Historical development of civil liberties in the United States

Throughout the history of the United States, the development of civil liberties has been a cornerstone of the nation's democratic principles. From the founding fathers' vision of individual rights to the ongoing struggle for equality, the evolution of civil liberties has shaped the nation's identity and values. This subchapter will explore the historical context and key milestones that have contributed to the protection and expansion of civil liberties in the United States.

The origins of civil liberties can be traced back to the drafting of the United States Constitution in 1787. The Bill of Rights, ratified in 1791, enshrined fundamental freedoms such as freedom of speech, religion, and the right to a fair trial. These constitutional protections formed the basis for the future development of civil liberties.

In the 19th century, the struggle for civil liberties gained momentum through movements such as abolitionism and women's suffrage. The Civil War and Reconstruction era further expanded civil rights with the enactment of the 13th, 14th, and 15th Amendments, which abolished slavery, granted equal protection under the law, and granted voting rights regardless of race.

The 20th century witnessed significant advancements in civil liberties. The Progressive Era saw the expansion of freedom of speech and the right to assemble, leading to landmark Supreme Court cases such as Schenck v. United States (1919) and Brandenburg v. Ohio (1969), which established the boundaries of free speech.

The Civil Rights Movement of the 1950s and 1960s brought about significant changes in civil liberties, particularly for African Americans. The Civil Rights Act of 1964 and the Voting Rights Act of 1965 outlawed racial discrimination and ensured voting rights for all citizens. These legislative victories marked a turning point in the fight for equality and expanded civil liberties for marginalized communities.

However, the post-9/11 era posed new challenges to civil liberties. The USA PATRIOT Act, enacted in response to the terrorist attacks, granted the government sweeping surveillance powers, raising concerns about privacy and individual rights. This subchapter will delve into the impact of the USA PATRIOT Act on civil liberties, examining the balance between national security and individual freedoms.

Understanding the historical development of civil liberties is crucial to analyzing the impact of the USA PATRIOT Act on individual rights and privacy. By examining the struggles and triumphs of the past, we can better navigate the complexities of the present and shape the future of civil liberties in the United States.

Key principles underlying civil liberties

In order to fully comprehend the impact of the USA PATRIOT Act on civil liberties, it is crucial to understand the key principles that underlie these fundamental rights. Civil liberties are the basic rights and freedoms that every individual possesses as a member of a democratic society. These principles serve as the foundation upon which a just and equitable society is built, ensuring that individuals are protected from government intrusion and arbitrary actions.

1. Individual Rights: The protection of individual rights lies at the core of civil liberties. These rights include freedom of speech, assembly, religion, and the press, as well as the right to privacy and due process. They are essential for cultivating a free and diverse society, allowing individuals to express themselves, pursue their beliefs, and live without unwarranted interference.

2. Limited Government Power: Civil liberties are based on the principle that government power should be limited and checked to prevent abuse and protect the rights of individuals. This principle ensures that the government does not overreach its authority or infringe upon the rights of its citizens without proper justification.

3. Rule of Law: Civil liberties are safeguarded by the rule of law, which means that all individuals, including government officials, are subject to the law and no one is above it. The rule of law ensures that legal

procedures are followed, protecting individuals from arbitrary actions and ensuring fair treatment for all.

4. Balancing Security and Liberty: Protecting civil liberties does not mean neglecting national security concerns. It is important to strike a balance between the need for security and the preservation of individual rights. While security measures may be necessary to safeguard the nation, they should not unduly infringe upon civil liberties without justification.

5. Transparency and Accountability: Civil liberties thrive in an environment of transparency and accountability. Government actions should be transparent, allowing citizens to hold their representatives accountable for their decisions. This accountability ensures that civil liberties are protected and that any infringements are subject to scrutiny and challenge.

Understanding these key principles underlying civil liberties provides a framework for critically evaluating the impact of the USA PATRIOT Act. It allows us to examine the extent to which this legislation has upheld or encroached upon these principles, and the subsequent effects on individual rights and privacy.

By analyzing the USA PATRIOT Act through the lens of these key principles, we can engage in a comprehensive discussion about the delicate balance between national security and civil liberties. This examination is crucial for all members of society, including students, academics, policy makers, journalists, and the general public, as it enables us to fully grasp the implications of this legislation and its impact on individual freedoms.

Chapter 3: Overview of the USA PATRIOT Act

Enactment and legislative history

Enactment and Legislative History: Understanding the Journey of the USA PATRIOT Act

The USA PATRIOT Act, officially known as the Uniting and Strengthening America by Providing Appropriate Tools Required to Intercept and Obstruct Terrorism Act, is a legislation that was enacted in response to the tragic events of September 11, 2001. This subchapter aims to shed light on the process of enacting the act and delve into its legislative history, providing a comprehensive understanding of its origins and development.

The USA PATRIOT Act was signed into law by President George W. Bush on October 26, 2001. However, its journey began shortly after the 9/11 attacks when policymakers and government officials realized the urgent need for enhanced tools to combat terrorism. The act was introduced to Congress just six weeks after the attacks, which showcases the speed at which it was developed and passed.

To fully comprehend the legislative history of the USA PATRIOT Act, it is essential to examine the debates and discussions that took place during its formulation. These discussions revolved around striking a delicate balance between national security and the protection of civil liberties. Lawmakers grappled with the question of how to empower law enforcement agencies to prevent future terrorist acts, while simultaneously ensuring the preservation of individual rights and privacy.

Throughout its legislative journey, the USA PATRIOT Act underwent various amendments and revisions. These changes were a result of both public and political pressure to address concerns about potential abuse of power and infringements on civil liberties. The act was subject to rigorous scrutiny, with advocates arguing for its necessity in the face of an evolving terrorist threat, while opponents voiced concerns over its potential to overreach and violate individual rights.

Understanding the legislative history of the USA PATRIOT Act is crucial for comprehending its impact on civil liberties. By tracing its origins and evolution, we can gain insights into the intentions behind its provisions and the subsequent effects on individual rights and privacy. This subchapter serves as a vital guide for researchers, policymakers, academics, and the general public alike, enabling them to navigate the complex landscape of the USA PATRIOT Act and its implications.

In conclusion, the enactment and legislative history of the USA PATRIOT Act offer a fascinating journey into the development of this significant legislation. By analyzing the debates and revisions that occurred during its formulation, we can better understand the delicate balance between national security and the preservation of civil liberties. This subchapter serves as a valuable resource for anyone seeking to explore the origins and impact of the USA PATRIOT Act, from students and researchers to policymakers and the general public.

Objectives and provisions of the Act

The USA PATRIOT Act, officially known as the Uniting and Strengthening America by Providing Appropriate Tools Required to Intercept and Obstruct Terrorism Act, was enacted on October 26, 2001, in response to the 9/11 terrorist attacks. This subchapter aims to provide an in-depth analysis of the objectives and provisions of the Act, focusing on its impact on civil liberties.

The primary objective of the USA PATRIOT Act was to enhance the government's ability to prevent and investigate acts of terrorism. It aimed to accomplish this by expanding the powers of law enforcement and intelligence agencies, improving information sharing between them, and strengthening surveillance and intelligence gathering capabilities. The Act granted greater authority to agencies such as the Federal Bureau of Investigation (FBI), allowing them to access a wider range of records and conduct surveillance on suspected terrorists or individuals associated with terrorism.

One of the key provisions of the Act was the expansion of surveillance powers under the Foreign Intelligence Surveillance Act (FISA). This allowed intelligence agencies to obtain warrants for surveillance and wiretapping in cases related to national security, including investigations into international terrorism. However, critics argue that this provision encroaches upon individual privacy rights and may lead to unwarranted government intrusion.

The Act also introduced the controversial provision of "sneak and peek" warrants, allowing law enforcement agencies to conduct searches without immediately notifying the target individual. Supporters argue that this provision is crucial in preventing the destruction of evidence and ensuring the safety of law enforcement personnel. However, opponents argue that it violates the Fourth Amendment, which protects against unreasonable searches and seizures.

Furthermore, the USA PATRIOT Act expanded the scope of the government's access to personal and business records, including financial and communication records. This provision aims to facilitate intelligence gathering and investigations into potential terrorist activities. However, concerns have been raised about the potential abuse of this power, as it may infringe upon individual privacy rights and result in unwarranted surveillance of innocent individuals.

In conclusion, the USA PATRIOT Act was enacted with the objective of enhancing the government's ability to prevent and investigate acts of terrorism. While supporters argue that the Act is crucial in ensuring national security, critics raise concerns about its impact on civil liberties, particularly individual rights and privacy. This subchapter aims to provide a comprehensive analysis of the Act's provisions and their implications on civil liberties, catering to a diverse audience including students, academics, policymakers, journalists, and the general public.

Controversies surrounding the Act

The USA PATRIOT Act, passed in response to the 9/11 terrorist attacks, has been a subject of intense debate and controversy since its enactment. This subchapter delves into the various controversies surrounding the Act, highlighting the concerns raised by critics and examining their impact on civil liberties.

One of the primary controversies surrounding the USA PATRIOT Act is the potential infringement on individual rights and privacy. Critics argue that the Act grants broad surveillance powers to the government, enabling the collection of personal data and monitoring of individuals without sufficient checks and balances. They argue that this violates the Fourth Amendment protection against unreasonable searches and seizures.

Another controversy lies in the Act's provisions regarding the sharing of information between law enforcement agencies and intelligence agencies. Critics argue that the Act encourages the sharing of sensitive information without adequate oversight, potentially leading to the misuse of information and the erosion of privacy rights. They raise concerns about the lack of transparency and accountability in the sharing of information under the Act.

Furthermore, critics argue that the Act undermines the principle of due process. They highlight provisions that allow for the detention of individuals suspected of terrorist activities without proper judicial oversight or access to legal representation. This, they argue, undermines the fundamental right to a fair trial and opens the door to potential abuses of power.

The Act has also faced criticism for its impact on immigrant communities. Critics argue that the Act's provisions, such as the expansion of surveillance of non-U.S. citizens and the broadening of immigration enforcement powers, disproportionately target and negatively impact immigrant communities. This has raised concerns about racial and ethnic profiling and the erosion of civil rights for non-U.S. citizens.

Finally, concerns have been raised about the chilling effect the Act may have on free speech and dissent. Critics argue that the Act's provisions, such as the expansion of surveillance powers and the broad definition of domestic terrorism, have the potential to stifle political dissent and discourage individuals from exercising their First Amendment rights.

It is essential to critically examine these controversies surrounding the USA PATRIOT Act to assess its impact on civil liberties. By understanding these concerns, policymakers, academics, and the general public can engage in informed discussions and work towards a balance between national security and the preservation of individual rights and privacy.

Chapter 4: Surveillance and Privacy Rights

Expansion of surveillance powers under the USA PATRIOT Act

The USA PATRIOT Act, enacted in the aftermath of the 9/11 terrorist attacks, has been a subject of intense debate and scrutiny regarding its impact on civil liberties. One of the most controversial aspects of the Act is the expansion of surveillance powers granted to intelligence agencies and law enforcement, which has raised concerns about the erosion of individual rights and privacy.

Under the provisions of the USA PATRIOT Act, government agencies such as the National Security Agency (NSA) and the Federal Bureau of Investigation (FBI) have been granted broader authority to conduct surveillance activities. This includes the ability to collect and analyze vast amounts of data, including phone records, emails, financial transactions, and internet usage, without the need for a warrant or probable cause. These powers have sparked concerns about the potential for unchecked government surveillance and the infringement of citizens' privacy rights.

Critics argue that the expansion of surveillance powers under the USA PATRIOT Act has led to a surveillance state, where the government has unprecedented access to personal information, monitoring activities, and private communications of individuals. This has raised fears of a chilling effect on freedom of speech and expression, as people might self-censor in the face of constant surveillance.

Moreover, the lack of transparency and oversight surrounding these surveillance activities has further exacerbated concerns. The secretive nature of surveillance programs, such as the NSA's mass data collection program, known as PRISM, has led to questions about the legality and constitutionality of these practices. Whistleblowers like Edward

Snowden have exposed the extent of government surveillance, triggering a global debate on privacy and civil liberties.

The impact of expanded surveillance powers also extends to marginalized communities, who may bear the brunt of profiling and discriminatory practices. Racial and religious minorities, activists, and journalists have expressed concerns about being targeted based on their ethnicity, political beliefs, or affiliations, leading to a climate of fear and suspicion.

In conclusion, the expansion of surveillance powers under the USA PATRIOT Act has had significant implications for civil liberties, individual rights, and privacy. The Act's provisions have allowed for extensive government surveillance without adequate checks and balances, raising legitimate concerns about the erosion of democratic values. As policymakers, researchers, and the general public, it is crucial to critically examine and evaluate the impact of these surveillance powers to ensure the protection of civil liberties in the face of national security concerns.

Implications for privacy rights and personal freedoms

In recent years, the USA PATRIOT Act has become a topic of intense debate and scrutiny, particularly with regards to its implications for privacy rights and personal freedoms. This subchapter aims to delve into the impact of this controversial legislation, examining its effects on civil liberties and shedding light on the potential consequences for individuals and society as a whole.

The USA PATRIOT Act, enacted in the aftermath of the 9/11 attacks, was designed to enhance national security and combat terrorism. However, critics argue that it has resulted in an erosion of privacy rights and an infringement on personal freedoms. One of the key concerns raised by civil liberties advocates is the Act's expanded surveillance powers, which allow government agencies to collect and analyze vast amounts of personal data without sufficient oversight.

Under the Act, intelligence agencies can access personal records, including medical, financial, and educational information, without obtaining a warrant. This has raised concerns about the potential for abuse and misuse of such sensitive data, as well as the chilling effect it may have on free expression and dissent. The Act also grants law enforcement agencies the authority to conduct secret searches and install surveillance devices without notifying the target individual, further exacerbating privacy concerns.

Furthermore, the Act has given rise to the controversial practice of "national security letters" (NSLs), which allow the FBI to demand information from organizations, such as internet service providers, libraries, and bookstores, without judicial oversight. Critics argue that this provision undermines the right to privacy and violates the Fourth Amendment protection against unreasonable searches and seizures.

The implications of the USA PATRIOT Act on personal freedoms extend beyond surveillance and data collection. The Act has also expanded the government's power to detain and investigate individuals suspected of terrorist activities, including U.S. citizens. This has raised concerns about due process and the right to a fair trial, as some individuals have been held indefinitely without being charged or given access to legal representation.

In conclusion, the USA PATRIOT Act has had far-reaching implications for privacy rights and personal freedoms. While its supporters argue that it is necessary for national security, critics contend that it infringes upon civil liberties and undermines the core values of a democratic society. Understanding the impact of this legislation is crucial for individuals, policymakers, and society at large, as it prompts important discussions about the balance between security and individual rights.

Case studies and real-life examples of privacy violations

Introduction:

The USA PATRIOT Act, enacted in the wake of the 9/11 terrorist attacks, has been a subject of intense debate due to its impact on civil liberties, particularly individual privacy. This subchapter delves into case studies and real-life examples that shed light on the privacy violations resulting from the implementation of this controversial legislation.

Case Study 1: Edward Snowden and the NSA Surveillance Program

Edward Snowden, a former National Security Agency (NSA) contractor, leaked classified documents in 2013, revealing the extent of the NSA's surveillance activities. These revelations exposed the mass collection of metadata, including phone records and internet communications of millions of Americans, without their knowledge or consent. This case study highlights the violation of privacy rights and the erosion of individual liberties that occurred under the USA PATRIOT Act.

Case Study 2: National Security Letters (NSLs) and Gag Orders

The use of National Security Letters (NSLs) by the FBI has come under scrutiny for their potential infringement on civil liberties. NSLs allow the FBI to secretly gather personal information, such as financial records, without obtaining a warrant or judicial oversight. The accompanying gag orders prevent individuals or organizations from disclosing the receipt of such letters, impeding transparency and accountability.

Case Study 3: Racial and Religious Profiling

The USA PATRIOT Act has been criticized for enabling racial and religious profiling, particularly targeting Muslim and Arab communities.

The case study examines instances where innocent individuals have been subjected to unwarranted surveillance, interrogations, and detentions solely based on their ethnicity or religious background. These violations not only infringe upon privacy rights but also perpetuate discrimination and xenophobia.

Real-life Example 1: The FBI's "Going Dark" Controversy

The FBI has argued that encryption technologies used by tech companies hinder their ability to investigate potential threats. This has led to clashes between privacy advocates and law enforcement agencies. This example explores the debate surrounding encryption and the potential impact on individual privacy, as well as the broader implications for national security and civil liberties.

Real-life Example 2: Corporate Data Breaches and Privacy Violations

Numerous high-profile data breaches, such as the Equifax breach in 2017, have exposed the personal information of millions of individuals. This real-life example showcases how weak privacy safeguards and inadequate regulation can lead to significant privacy violations. It highlights the need for comprehensive data protection laws that balance individual privacy rights with the legitimate needs of businesses and national security.

Conclusion:

These case studies and real-life examples illuminate the alarming privacy violations resulting from the implementation of the USA PATRIOT Act. They underscore the urgent need for robust safeguards, oversight mechanisms, and informed public discourse to strike a balance between security concerns and the protection of civil liberties. Understanding these violations is crucial for policymakers, journalists, academics, and the general public in order to engage in informed discussions and shape policies that preserve individual rights and privacy in the face of evolving security challenges.

Chapter 5: Impact on Freedom of Speech and Expression

Examination of the Act's provisions related to free speech

The USA PATRIOT Act, enacted in the wake of the 9/11 attacks, has been a subject of intense scrutiny and debate due to its potential impact on civil liberties. One of the key areas of concern is the Act's provisions related to free speech, as it raises questions about the balance between national security and individual rights.

Under the Act, several provisions empower law enforcement agencies to monitor and investigate individuals suspected of engaging in terrorist activities. While these measures aim to prevent future attacks, they have raised concerns about potential infringements on free speech rights. Critics argue that the Act's broad language and expansive powers may lead to the suppression of dissenting voices and the chilling effect on public discourse.

Section 215 of the Act, commonly referred to as the "library provision," grants authorities the power to obtain records and other tangible items related to national security investigations. This provision has been criticized for its potential to infringe on the privacy of individuals and their right to free expression. The fear that individuals may self-censor their reading habits out of fear of being targeted has raised concerns among librarians, educators, and intellectuals.

Furthermore, the Act's provision on material support for terrorism has been a contentious issue when it comes to free speech. The government has the authority to prosecute individuals who provide any form of assistance to organizations designated as terrorist groups. While this provision aims to cut off support for terrorism, it raises questions about the potential criminalization of speech and association, particularly in cases where individuals may unknowingly support a designated organization.

The Act's provisions related to electronic surveillance also have implications for free speech. The controversial provision known as the "roving wiretap" expands the government's ability to monitor communications, including phone calls, emails, and internet browsing history. Critics argue that this provision, coupled with the lack of transparency and accountability, poses a threat to the privacy of individuals and their ability to freely express themselves online.

In conclusion, the provisions of the USA PATRIOT Act related to free speech have generated significant concerns about the potential infringement on civil liberties. While national security is undoubtedly crucial, it is essential to strike a balance that protects individual rights and preserves the vibrancy of public discourse. Understanding the impact of these provisions is crucial for policymakers, government officials, academics, journalists, and the general public as they navigate the complex landscape of civil liberties in the post-9/11 era.

Analysis of First Amendment implications

The First Amendment of the United States Constitution guarantees several fundamental rights, including freedom of speech, press, religion, assembly, and the right to petition the government. These rights are crucial pillars of democracy and have long been considered the bedrock of American society. However, since the passage of the USA PATRIOT Act, concerns have been raised about the potential implications for these First Amendment rights.

One of the key areas of concern is freedom of speech. The USA PATRIOT Act grants law enforcement agencies broader powers to monitor and investigate potential threats to national security. While this is important for protecting the country, there is a risk that these expanded powers may be used to suppress dissenting voices and stifle free speech. Critics argue that the Act's provisions, such as the authority to conduct "roving wiretaps" and access to library and bookstore records, could have a chilling effect on individuals and organizations who fear being targeted for their political or religious beliefs.

Similarly, freedom of the press may also be at risk. The Act includes provisions that allow the government to obtain certain records, including those held by news organizations, without the need for a warrant. This raises concerns about the potential for government interference in journalistic activities and the protection of confidential sources. Journalists argue that these provisions undermine their ability to report on matters of public interest without fear of reprisal or surveillance.

Religious freedom is another area that has been scrutinized in relation to the USA PATRIOT Act. The Act grants the government the authority to monitor religious institutions and organizations suspected of being involved in terrorist activities. While it is important to protect national security, there are concerns that this provision could lead to the targeting and profiling of certain religious communities, infringing upon their right to freely practice their faith without fear of discrimination or surveillance.

The right to peacefully assemble and petition the government may also be affected by the Act. Critics argue that the broad surveillance powers granted to law enforcement agencies could deter individuals from participating in protests or political gatherings, out of fear of being monitored or labeled as potential threats to national security. This could have a chilling effect on the ability of citizens to exercise their First Amendment rights to express their grievances and advocate for change.

In conclusion, the USA PATRIOT Act has raised significant concerns regarding its potential implications for First Amendment rights. While the Act aims to enhance national security, it is crucial to carefully balance these objectives with the protection of civil liberties. A robust and ongoing analysis of the Act's impact on individual rights and privacy is necessary to ensure that the First Amendment continues to be safeguarded in the face of evolving security threats.

Consequences for dissent and government criticism

The USA PATRIOT Act, enacted in the aftermath of the September 11 attacks, has generated extensive debate and concern regarding its impact on civil liberties, particularly in relation to dissent and government criticism. This subchapter aims to analyze the consequences of the Act on individuals who express dissenting views or criticize the government, shedding light on the potential threats to freedom of speech and expression.

One of the primary concerns arising from the USA PATRIOT Act is the expansion of surveillance powers granted to law enforcement agencies. Under the Act, the government can now monitor individuals' communication activities, including phone calls, emails, and internet browsing, without requiring a warrant or demonstrating probable cause. This broad surveillance authority has raised fears of government overreach and potential abuse, particularly when it comes to individuals expressing dissenting opinions or criticizing governmental actions. The Act's provisions have the potential to create a chilling effect, deterring individuals from freely expressing their views due to the fear of being targeted for surveillance or retaliation.

Moreover, the Act has also had implications for academic freedom and research. For scholars, researchers, and students, the fear of government scrutiny and potential consequences for engaging in dissent or criticism can hinder the pursuit of knowledge and the free exchange of ideas. This can stifle academic discourse and limit the exploration of critical perspectives, undermining the foundation of a democratic society that thrives on diverse viewpoints.

Additionally, the USA PATRIOT Act has had an impact on the media and journalism. Journalists and reporters who investigate and report on government activities or national security issues may find themselves targeted under the Act's provisions. The Act's broad definitions of "domestic terrorism" and "material support" have raised concerns that journalists engaging in investigative reporting or whistleblowing activities may be subjected to surveillance or even criminal charges. This can have a chilling effect on investigative journalism, impeding the ability to hold the government accountable and limiting the public's access to vital information.

In conclusion, the consequences of the USA PATRIOT Act on dissent and government criticism are significant. The Act's broad surveillance powers, coupled with its potential implications for academic freedom and journalism, pose a threat to civil liberties and the fundamental principles of democracy. It is imperative for policymakers, academics, journalists, and the general public to critically examine these consequences and engage in open dialogue to ensure the preservation of individual rights and privacy in the face of national security concerns.

Chapter 6: Racial and Religious Profiling

Discussion on discriminatory practices authorized by the Act

The USA PATRIOT Act, passed in the wake of the September 11th terrorist attacks, is a legislation that has had a significant impact on civil liberties in the United States. While its primary objective was to enhance national security and prevent future acts of terrorism, there have been concerns raised about the potential for discriminatory practices authorized by the Act.

One of the key provisions of the USA PATRIOT Act that has been criticized for its potential to foster discriminatory practices is Section 215, which grants the government the power to obtain "any tangible thing" deemed relevant to an ongoing investigation. Critics argue that this provision allows for the indiscriminate collection of personal information, including library records, without sufficient oversight or probable cause. This has raised concerns among individuals and groups who fear that their privacy rights are being violated, particularly those belonging to minority communities who have historically been targets of discrimination.

Another provision that has been subject to scrutiny is Section 213, commonly known as the "sneak and peek" provision. This allows law enforcement agencies to conduct searches without immediately notifying the target individual or organization. Critics argue that this provision not only infringes upon the Fourth Amendment protection against unreasonable searches and seizures but also opens the door for potential abuse and profiling of certain individuals or communities based on their race, religion, or ethnicity.

Additionally, the USA PATRIOT Act has provisions that grant the government broad surveillance powers, such as the ability to obtain roving wiretaps and conduct surveillance on "lone wolf" individuals who are not affiliated with any known terrorist organization. While these measures were meant to enhance national security, there are concerns that they may disproportionately target and infringe upon the civil liberties of innocent individuals, particularly those from marginalized communities.

It is essential to critically examine and discuss these discriminatory practices authorized by the USA PATRIOT Act to ensure that civil liberties are protected for all individuals, regardless of their race, religion, or ethnicity. By engaging in these discussions, we can evaluate the impact of the Act on individual rights and privacy and identify potential areas for reform. It is crucial for policymakers, government officials, and all members of society to be aware of the potential discriminatory consequences of such legislation to uphold the principles of fairness, justice, and equality that are fundamental to a democratic society.

Examination of the impact on marginalized communities

The USA PATRIOT Act, enacted in response to the 9/11 terrorist attacks, has been a subject of intense debate and scrutiny since its inception. While the Act aimed to enhance national security, there have been concerns about its potential impact on civil liberties, particularly for marginalized communities. This subchapter delves into the examination of the Act's impact on these communities and sheds light on the consequences it has had on their rights and privacy.

Marginalized communities, including racial and ethnic minorities, immigrants, religious minorities, and low-income individuals, have historically faced systemic discrimination and unequal treatment. The implementation of the USA PATRIOT Act has further exacerbated these inequalities, as it has provided law enforcement agencies with expanded surveillance powers and the ability to infringe upon individual rights without sufficient checks and balances.

One key area of concern is the Act's provisions related to racial and ethnic profiling. Critics argue that the Act has disproportionately targeted individuals from Muslim, Arab, and South Asian backgrounds, leading to increased surveillance, racial profiling, and discrimination. This has not only violated the rights of innocent individuals but has also created a climate of fear and mistrust within these communities.

Furthermore, the Act has expanded the government's authority to collect and analyze personal data, including financial, medical, and educational records, without adequate oversight. This has raised concerns about the violation of privacy rights, particularly for marginalized individuals who already face heightened scrutiny and surveillance.

In addition to these direct impacts, the Act has also had indirect consequences on marginalized communities. The fear of being targeted or monitored has led to self-censorship and limited freedom of expression within these communities. It has also contributed to the erosion of trust between law enforcement agencies and marginalized communities, hindering effective cooperation in combating terrorism.

To address these concerns, it is crucial for policymakers, government officials, and the general public to critically examine the impact of the USA PATRIOT Act on marginalized communities. It is imperative to strike a balance between ensuring national security and safeguarding civil liberties for all individuals, regardless of their background or social status.

By understanding the specific challenges faced by marginalized communities and the ways in which the Act has affected their rights and privacy, policymakers can work towards amending and refining legislation to ensure equal protection and justice for all. It is also essential for the general public, academics, researchers, and civil society organizations to remain vigilant and advocate for the protection of civil liberties, particularly for those who are most vulnerable.

Legal challenges and ethical considerations

The USA PATRIOT Act, enacted in the wake of the 9/11 terrorist attacks, has had far-reaching implications for civil liberties and individual rights. This subchapter delves into the legal challenges and ethical considerations arising from the implementation of this controversial legislation.

One of the primary legal challenges posed by the USA PATRIOT Act lies in the tension between national security and the protection of civil liberties. Critics argue that the Act grants the government unprecedented powers that potentially infringe upon constitutional rights, such as the Fourth Amendment's protection against unreasonable searches and seizures. The provision allowing for the collection of business records and the roving wiretap provision have drawn particular scrutiny, as they enable surveillance without sufficient judicial oversight. These provisions raise concerns about the potential for abuse and the erosion of privacy rights.

Ethical considerations surrounding the USA PATRIOT Act revolve around the balance between security and individual freedom. The Act's proponents argue that the enhanced surveillance powers are necessary to combat terrorism effectively. However, critics contend that the Act places undue emphasis on security at the expense of civil liberties, potentially leading to a surveillance state. The ethical dilemma lies in determining the appropriate trade-off between security and privacy, and ensuring that the government's actions are proportionate and justified.

Another legal challenge centers on the Act's impact on immigrant communities. The USA PATRIOT Act expanded the government's authority to detain and deport individuals suspected of terrorism-related activities. However, this broadened power has raised concerns about racial profiling and the potential for abuse targeting specific ethnic or religious groups. The question of whether these provisions violate the equal protection rights enshrined in the Constitution has been a subject of legal debate.

From an ethical standpoint, the Act's impact on civil liberties extends beyond its direct provisions. It has created a climate of fear and suspicion, leading to increased stigmatization and discrimination against certain communities. These ethical considerations prompt a broader discussion on the responsibility of the government to protect both national security and the principles of inclusivity and equal treatment for all.

In conclusion, the legal challenges and ethical considerations surrounding the USA PATRIOT Act are of paramount importance in understanding its impact on civil liberties and individual rights. Properly addressing these concerns requires a thoughtful examination of the Act's provisions and their potential ramifications. As a society, we must strive to strike a balance between security and the preservation of civil liberties, ensuring that our actions align with our democratic principles and values.

Chapter 7: Due Process and the Rule of Law

Analysis of the Act's impact on due process rights

The USA PATRIOT Act, enacted in the wake of the 9/11 attacks, has been a subject of intense debate and scrutiny, particularly regarding its impact on due process rights. This subchapter aims to provide a comprehensive analysis of how the Act has affected these fundamental rights, and the implications it holds for civil liberties.

One of the key provisions of the Act that has drawn criticism is the expanded power granted to law enforcement agencies in conducting surveillance and gathering intelligence. Under Section 215, the government can obtain "tangible things" such as business records and library records without demonstrating probable cause. This provision has raised concerns about the potential violation of due process rights, as it allows for the collection of personal information without the need for a warrant. Critics argue that this provision infringes upon individuals' rights to privacy and challenges the principles of due process.

Another area of concern is the "Sneak and Peek" provision, which allows law enforcement agencies to conduct searches without immediately notifying the target individual. While proponents argue that this provision is necessary to combat terrorism and protect national security, others argue that it undermines the principle of due process by denying individuals the opportunity to challenge the search in a timely manner.

Additionally, the Act has expanded the use of National Security Letters (NSLs), which enable the FBI to compel businesses and organizations to provide customer records and other sensitive information without judicial oversight. Critics argue that the lack of judicial review in the NSL process undermines due process rights, as individuals have no opportunity to challenge the government's requests for their personal information.

Furthermore, the Act has broadened the definition of "domestic terrorism," which has led to concerns about the potential for abuse and infringement on First Amendment rights. Critics argue that the Act's language is overly broad and allows for the targeting of individuals or groups engaged in constitutionally protected activities, thus violating due process rights.

In conclusion, the USA PATRIOT Act has had a significant impact on due process rights in the United States. While proponents argue that these measures are necessary for national security, critics contend that the Act infringes upon civil liberties and undermines the principles of due process. It is essential for policymakers, academics, and the general public to critically analyze the Act's impact on due process rights to ensure a balance between national security and the protection of civil liberties.

Critiques of the Act's disregard for legal safeguards

One of the most significant concerns surrounding the USA PATRIOT Act is its disregard for legal safeguards that have long been considered fundamental to protecting civil liberties. Critics argue that the Act's provisions grant excessive powers to law enforcement agencies and intelligence organizations, potentially infringing upon the rights of individuals and undermining the principles of due process and privacy.

First and foremost, critics argue that the Act's broad definition of terrorism and its expansion of surveillance powers have led to increased government intrusion into the lives of innocent civilians. The Act allows law enforcement agencies to conduct surveillance on individuals without requiring evidence of criminal activity, merely on the suspicion of involvement in terrorism-related activities. This has raised concerns that innocent individuals may be subjected to unwarranted surveillance, leading to a chilling effect on free speech and association.

Furthermore, the Act grants law enforcement agencies the authority to conduct searches and seizures without prior notification and without obtaining a warrant. This provision, known as the "sneak and peek" provision, allows law enforcement to enter and search private property without the knowledge or consent of the owner. Critics argue that this undermines the Fourth Amendment protections against unreasonable searches and seizures, eroding the balance between individual rights and national security.

The Act also expands the use of National Security Letters (NSLs), which allow the FBI to obtain sensitive personal information, such as financial records and internet browsing history, without a court order. Critics argue that the use of NSLs bypasses the traditional checks and balances of the judicial system, potentially leading to abuse and the violation of privacy rights.

Moreover, critics highlight the Act's provision that allows the sharing of intelligence information between law enforcement agencies and intelligence organizations, including foreign governments. This broad sharing of information raises concerns about the lack of oversight and accountability, potentially leading to the targeting of innocent individuals based on erroneous or unreliable intelligence.

In conclusion, critiques of the USA PATRIOT Act's disregard for legal safeguards focus on the potential infringements on individual rights and privacy. Critics argue that the Act's provisions grant excessive powers to law enforcement agencies, eroding fundamental principles of due process and undermining the balance between national security and civil liberties. It is crucial to examine the impact of these provisions on individual rights and privacy to ensure that the Act does not compromise the very foundations upon which our democracy is built.

Case studies illustrating erosion of the rule of law

Introduction:

The erosion of the rule of law is a deeply concerning issue that has raised alarms among civil liberties advocates and scholars. This subchapter aims to shed light on the impact of the USA PATRIOT Act on civil liberties by examining a series of case studies. By delving into these real-life examples, we can better understand how the rule of law has been undermined, leading to potential infringements on individual rights and privacy.

Case Study 1: The Ahmed case

In 2007, the case of Syed Fahad Hashmi, also known as Ahmed, grabbed headlines. Ahmed, a US citizen, was subjected to extraordinary rendition and held in solitary confinement for three years without trial. Under the USA PATRIOT Act, the government had the power to detain individuals suspected of terrorism indefinitely. This case highlighted the erosion of due process and the denial of habeas corpus rights.

Case Study 2: The Smith case

In 2013, the revelations made by Edward Snowden exposed the extent of surveillance authorized by the USA PATRIOT Act. The case of James Smith, an ordinary American citizen, highlighted the chilling effect of government surveillance on individual privacy rights. Smith, unaware that his communications were being monitored, faced severe consequences when his private conversations were used against him in court, violating his Fourth Amendment rights.

Case Study 3: The Al-Marri case

Ali Saleh Kahlah Al-Marri, a legal resident of the United States, was arrested in 2001 as a suspected terrorist. Under the USA PATRIOT Act,

Al-Marri was held in military custody as an enemy combatant without charges or access to legal representation. This case revealed the erosion of habeas corpus rights and demonstrated the potential for abuse when the rule of law is compromised.

Case Study 4: The Muhtorov case

In 2012, Jamshid Muhtorov, a refugee from Uzbekistan, was arrested under suspicion of providing material support to a terrorist organization. The case highlighted the broad interpretation of the USA PATRIOT Act, allowing the government to label individuals as terrorists based on vague criteria. Muhtorov's case raised concerns about the erosion of free speech rights and the potential for wrongful convictions.

Conclusion:

Through these case studies, it becomes evident that the USA PATRIOT Act has had a significant impact on civil liberties, particularly in terms of erosion of the rule of law. These examples underscore the importance of striking a balance between national security and individual rights. It is crucial for policymakers, academics, and the general public to critically analyze the implications of legislation such as the USA PATRIOT Act to safeguard civil liberties in an increasingly complex and interconnected world.

Chapter 8: Balancing National Security and Civil Liberties

Arguments for the necessity of the Act in safeguarding national security

The USA PATRIOT Act is a highly controversial legislation that was enacted shortly after the 9/11 terrorist attacks. While it has faced criticism for potentially infringing upon civil liberties, there are compelling arguments for its necessity in safeguarding national security. This subchapter aims to explore these arguments and shed light on the justifications behind the Act.

First and foremost, the USA PATRIOT Act equips law enforcement agencies with enhanced tools and capabilities to combat terrorism effectively. It grants broader surveillance powers, allowing intelligence agencies to monitor and track potential threats more efficiently. In an era where terrorist networks are becoming increasingly sophisticated and technologically advanced, it is crucial for authorities to keep pace with these evolving threats. By providing these agencies with the necessary tools, the Act enables them to gather intelligence and prevent potential attacks before they occur.

Furthermore, the Act promotes information sharing and cooperation between intelligence agencies, law enforcement, and other relevant entities. Prior to its enactment, there were significant barriers and restrictions on the exchange of critical information between different agencies. The USA PATRIOT Act removes these obstacles, facilitating swift and effective communication among various entities. This synergy is vital in identifying and neutralizing potential threats, as it enables a comprehensive and coordinated response to terrorism.

Moreover, the Act strengthens the legal framework necessary for prosecuting terrorists and their associates. It streamlines the process of obtaining search warrants, wiretaps, and other surveillance authorizations, making it easier for law enforcement to gather evidence and build strong cases against individuals involved in terrorist activities. This not only enables the justice system to hold terrorists accountable but also acts as a deterrent, sending a clear message that terrorism will not be tolerated.

Lastly, it is important to note that the USA PATRIOT Act contains numerous safeguards to prevent abuse of power and protect civil liberties. These include oversight mechanisms, such as judicial review and regular reporting requirements, ensuring that the enhanced powers granted under the Act are used responsibly and within the confines of the law.

In conclusion, while the USA PATRIOT Act has faced criticism for its potential impact on civil liberties, there are strong arguments for its necessity in safeguarding national security. By equipping law enforcement agencies with enhanced tools, promoting information sharing, and strengthening the legal framework for prosecuting terrorists, the Act plays a crucial role in preventing future attacks and ensuring the safety of the nation. However, it is essential to continually evaluate and balance the Act's provisions with the protection of individual rights and privacy, ensuring that the scales are not tipped too far in favor of security at the expense of civil liberties.

Evaluating the trade-offs between security and civil liberties

In today's complex and ever-changing world, the delicate balance between security and civil liberties has become a topic of great concern and debate. The USA PATRIOT Act, enacted in the aftermath of the September 11 attacks, has been at the forefront of this discussion. This subchapter aims to critically analyze the impact of the act on civil liberties, shedding light on the trade-offs that have been made in the name of national security.

The USA PATRIOT Act was introduced with the primary objective of enhancing the government's ability to prevent future terrorist attacks. It provided law enforcement agencies with expanded powers to gather intelligence, conduct surveillance, and share information, all in the interest of protecting national security. However, these increased powers have raised questions about their potential infringement on individual rights and privacy.

One of the key trade-offs between security and civil liberties lies in the balance between government surveillance and the right to privacy. The act granted authorities the authority to monitor communications, including phone calls and internet activities, without the need for a warrant. While this provision has undoubtedly helped in detecting and preventing terrorist activities, it has also raised concerns about the government's intrusion into the private lives of citizens.

Another trade-off can be seen in the erosion of due process rights. The act expanded the scope of surveillance and intelligence gathering, often without sufficient oversight or judicial review. This has led to cases of mistaken identity, wrongful detentions, and the potential for abuse of power. Balancing the need for swift action against potential threats with the preservation of individual rights has proven to be a challenge.

Furthermore, the act has had a chilling effect on freedom of expression and association. The broad definitions of terrorism and material support for terrorism have created a climate of fear, potentially stifling dissent and curtailing political activism. Critics argue that the act's provisions have had a chilling effect on civil liberties, undermining the very principles that the United States holds dear.

It is important to recognize that evaluating the trade-offs between security and civil liberties is a complex task. While the USA PATRIOT Act has undoubtedly played a role in preventing terrorist attacks and enhancing national security, it has also raised valid concerns about the erosion of civil liberties. Striking a balance between these two competing interests is crucial to maintaining a free and democratic society.

This subchapter aims to provide a comprehensive analysis of the impact of the USA PATRIOT Act on civil liberties, examining the potential trade-offs that have been made in the pursuit of security. By critically evaluating the act's provisions and their consequences, we hope to foster a better understanding of the challenges faced in preserving individual rights while ensuring the safety of the nation.

Alternative approaches to counterterrorism and protecting civil liberties

In recent years, counterterrorism efforts have become increasingly important in safeguarding national security. However, as governments implement measures to combat terrorism, concerns have been raised regarding the potential infringement on civil liberties and individual rights. This subchapter aims to explore alternative approaches to counterterrorism that strike a balance between ensuring public safety and protecting civil liberties.

One alternative approach to counterterrorism is the use of intelligence-led policing. This approach emphasizes the collection and analysis of information to identify and prevent terrorist activities. By focusing on intelligence rather than mass surveillance, intelligence-led policing allows for a more targeted and efficient approach, minimizing the potential for unnecessary intrusion into individuals' privacy. Additionally, this approach encourages cooperation and information sharing between law enforcement agencies, intelligence agencies, and the public, fostering a sense of trust and community engagement.

Another alternative approach is the promotion of community policing. Community policing encourages law enforcement agencies to work closely with local communities to identify and address security threats. By building strong relationships with community members, law enforcement agencies gain valuable insights into potential threats while also fostering a sense of trust and cooperation. This approach not only enhances public safety but also empowers communities to play an active role in countering terrorism and protecting civil liberties.

Furthermore, investing in education and awareness campaigns can be an effective alternative approach to counterterrorism. By promoting understanding and tolerance, these campaigns aim to address the root causes of extremism, such as social exclusion and ideological grievances. By focusing on prevention rather than solely on reactive measures, education and awareness campaigns can help create resilient societies that are less susceptible to radicalization.

Lastly, international cooperation and collaboration are essential in addressing the global threat of terrorism while safeguarding civil liberties. By sharing intelligence, best practices, and resources, nations can work together to combat terrorism without compromising individual rights. International agreements and frameworks, such as the United Nations Global Counter-Terrorism Strategy, provide a platform for countries to collaborate and coordinate their efforts, ensuring a comprehensive and rights-respecting approach to counterterrorism.

In conclusion, alternative approaches to counterterrorism exist that strike a balance between ensuring public safety and protecting civil liberties. Intelligence-led policing, community policing, education and awareness campaigns, and international cooperation all offer viable solutions to address the challenges of terrorism while respecting individual rights and privacy. By adopting these alternative approaches, governments can effectively combat terrorism while upholding the values and principles that underpin civil liberties.

Chapter 9: The Role of Oversight and Checks and Balances

Examination of oversight mechanisms for the Act

The USA PATRIOT Act, enacted in the wake of the September 11th attacks, significantly impacted civil liberties in the United States. As the title suggests, this subchapter delves into the examination of oversight mechanisms for this controversial legislation. It explores the systems put in place to ensure that the Act does not infringe upon individual rights and privacy, despite its broad powers granted to law enforcement agencies.

One of the primary oversight mechanisms established for the USA PATRIOT Act is the Foreign Intelligence Surveillance Court (FISC). This court was created to oversee government requests for surveillance warrants in cases involving national security. The subchapter provides a comprehensive analysis of the FISC's composition, procedures, and its role in safeguarding civil liberties. It critically examines whether the FISC strikes the right balance between protecting national security interests and preserving individual rights.

Additionally, the subchapter discusses the role of the Privacy and Civil Liberties Oversight Board (PCLOB). This independent agency was established to ensure that government actions, including those under the USA PATRIOT Act, do not violate privacy rights or civil liberties. The content explores the PCLOB's authority, composition, and its effectiveness in providing oversight and accountability. It delves into specific cases where the PCLOB has intervened to rectify potential abuses of power.

Furthermore, the subchapter examines the role of Congress in overseeing the Act. It analyzes the congressional committees responsible for conducting oversight, such as the House Judiciary Committee and the Senate Judiciary Committee. It discusses their powers, responsibilities, and their efforts to strike a balance between national security and civil liberties. The content also highlights instances where congressional oversight has resulted in amendments and reforms to mitigate the impact of the Act on individual rights.

Lastly, the subchapter critically evaluates the effectiveness of these oversight mechanisms. It examines the challenges faced by the FISC, PCLOB, and Congress in providing robust oversight. It explores potential weaknesses in the current system and proposes recommendations for strengthening oversight to better protect civil liberties.

This content is essential reading for undergraduate and graduate students, policymakers, journalists, and researchers seeking a comprehensive understanding of the USA PATRIOT Act, its impact on civil liberties, and the oversight mechanisms in place to safeguard individual rights and privacy. It offers insights and analysis that will foster informed discussions and debates among a diverse range of audiences, including government officials, military personnel, educators, and the general public.

Assessment of the effectiveness of oversight in protecting civil liberties

In the subchapter titled "Assessment of the Effectiveness of Oversight in Protecting Civil Liberties," we delve into a critical examination of the USA PATRIOT Act and its impact on individual rights and privacy. This section aims to provide a comprehensive assessment of the oversight mechanisms put in place to safeguard civil liberties.

The USA PATRIOT Act, enacted in response to the September 11, 2001 terrorist attacks, granted law enforcement agencies sweeping powers to combat terrorism. However, concerns arose regarding the potential abuse of these powers and their impact on civil liberties. To address these concerns, various oversight mechanisms were established to ensure accountability and protect individual rights.

This subchapter explores the effectiveness of these oversight mechanisms in achieving their intended goals. We analyze the role of Congress in overseeing the implementation of the PATRIOT Act, including the House and Senate committees responsible for reviewing its provisions. We scrutinize the extent to which these committees have exercised their oversight powers, evaluating the effectiveness of their efforts in protecting civil liberties.

Furthermore, we examine the role of the judiciary in overseeing the PATRIOT Act. The subchapter delves into the landmark court cases that have challenged the constitutionality of certain provisions, such as the controversial Section 215 allowing for the collection of bulk metadata. We assess the judiciary's effectiveness in striking a balance between national security concerns and the protection of civil liberties.

Additionally, we consider the role of non-governmental organizations (NGOs) and civil society in monitoring the PATRIOT Act's impact on civil liberties. We analyze the efforts of NGOs in advocating for transparency, accountability, and the protection of individual rights.

By critically evaluating the effectiveness of oversight mechanisms, this subchapter provides a comprehensive analysis of the extent to which civil liberties are protected under the USA PATRIOT Act. It offers valuable insights for undergraduate and graduate students, high school students, academics, researchers, policy makers, government officials, journalists, business professionals, military and defense personnel, think tanks, analysts, the general public, librarians, educators, non-government organizations, diplomats, international workers, and book clubs interested in understanding the impact of the PATRIOT Act on civil liberties.

In conclusion, this subchapter sheds light on the multifaceted nature of oversight in protecting civil liberties under the USA PATRIOT Act. It critically examines the effectiveness of oversight mechanisms, ensuring a nuanced understanding of the balance between national security and individual rights.

Recommendations for strengthening oversight and accountability

In order to address the concerns raised by the USA PATRIOT Act and its impact on civil liberties, it is essential to establish a robust system of oversight and accountability. This subchapter will outline key recommendations for strengthening oversight mechanisms and ensuring the protection of individual rights and privacy.

1. Enhancing Congressional Oversight: It is imperative that Congress plays a more active role in overseeing the implementation and enforcement of the USA PATRIOT Act. This can be achieved by establishing a dedicated committee or task force with the authority to review and assess the Act's impact on civil liberties. Regular hearings, reports, and audits should be conducted to ensure transparency and accountability.

2. Judicial Review: The role of the judiciary in safeguarding civil liberties cannot be understated. To enhance accountability, it is recommended that the scope of judicial review be expanded. This includes promoting greater scrutiny over surveillance activities, ensuring adequate checks and balances, and strengthening the process of obtaining warrants for searches and seizures.

3. Independent Oversight Bodies: The establishment of independent oversight bodies can provide an additional layer of accountability. These bodies should be granted the authority to investigate complaints, monitor the actions of law enforcement agencies, and report their

findings to the public. Transparent and unbiased investigations are crucial in upholding civil liberties.

4. Privacy Protection: Measures must be taken to protect individual privacy rights. This includes strict limitations on the collection, retention, and dissemination of personal information. Clear guidelines should be established to ensure that information is only accessed and used for legitimate national security purposes, preventing abuse and unwarranted intrusion into individuals' lives.

5.   Whistleblower   Protection: Encouraging   and   protecting whistleblowers is essential for maintaining accountability within government agencies. Implementing mechanisms to shield individuals who expose wrongdoing or violations of civil liberties will foster a culture of transparency and deter potential abuses.

6. Public Education and Awareness: It is important to educate and raise awareness among the general public about the implications of the USA PATRIOT Act on civil liberties. This can be achieved through public campaigns, educational programs, and community engagement initiatives. Increased knowledge and understanding will empower individuals to protect their rights and actively participate in the democratic process.

By implementing these recommendations, it is possible to strike a balance between national security and the protection of civil liberties. Strengthening oversight and accountability mechanisms will ensure that the USA PATRIOT Act is applied judiciously and in a manner consistent with the principles of democracy and individual rights.

Chapter 10: Public Perception and Debates

Analysis of public opinion on the USA PATRIOT Act

The USA PATRIOT Act, enacted in the aftermath of the 9/11 terrorist attacks, has been a topic of intense debate and scrutiny since its inception. This subchapter aims to delve into the analysis of public opinion surrounding this controversial legislation, providing valuable insights into the diverse perspectives on the Act's impact on civil liberties.

Understanding public opinion on the USA PATRIOT Act is crucial, as it allows us to gauge the perceptions and concerns of various stakeholders. This analysis encompasses the viewpoints of diverse groups, including undergraduate and graduate students, high school students, academics and researchers, policy makers and government officials, journalists, business professionals, military and defense personnel, think tanks and analysts, the general public, librarians and educators, non-government organizations, diplomats and international workers, and book clubs.

The chapter begins by highlighting the range of opinions expressed by high school and college students, who form a significant demographic affected by the Act's provisions. Drawing from surveys, interviews, and scholarly research, it explores how these young individuals perceive the balance between national security and civil liberties, shedding light on their concerns and expectations.

Next, the chapter examines the viewpoints of academics and researchers who have dedicated extensive studies to the USA PATRIOT Act. Their analyses provide an in-depth understanding of the Act's provisions, their implications on civil liberties, and potential areas for improvement. This segment also explores the debates and controversies surrounding the Act within academic circles.

The chapter further encompasses the perspectives of policy makers, government officials, and defense personnel who have either supported or criticized the USA PATRIOT Act. By examining their justifications, concerns, and proposed amendments, this analysis offers a comprehensive understanding of the Act's impact on national security and individual rights.

Additionally, the subchapter investigates the opinions expressed by journalists, business professionals, think tanks, and analysts, who often weigh the Act's implications from an economic, ethical, or geopolitical standpoint. Their insights provide valuable perspectives on the Act's implications for business operations, international relations, and media freedom.

Ultimately, the subchapter concludes by summarizing the general public's perception of the USA PATRIOT Act. By examining public opinion polls, social media trends, and grassroots activism, this analysis sheds light on the Act's support, opposition, and ongoing public discourse.

This comprehensive analysis of public opinion on the USA PATRIOT Act offers valuable insights for understanding the Act's impact on civil liberties. By exploring diverse perspectives, this subchapter aims to foster a nuanced understanding of the ongoing debates surrounding national security and individual rights in the United States.

Debates surrounding the Act's renewal and reform

As the USA PATRIOT Act approached its expiration date in 2015, a heated debate ensued regarding its renewal and the need for reform. This chapter delves into the key arguments put forth by various stakeholders, highlighting the concerns and justifications surrounding the Act's potential continuation.

Advocates for the renewal of the Act emphasized its importance in safeguarding national security in the post-9/11 era. They argued that the Act provided law enforcement agencies with vital tools to combat terrorism, such as enhanced surveillance capabilities, information sharing among intelligence agencies, and the ability to track and intercept communication among potential threats. These proponents contended that without the Act's provisions, the United States would be left vulnerable to future terrorist attacks, necessitating its renewal to ensure the safety of its citizens.

On the other side of the debate, critics raised serious concerns about the potential infringement on civil liberties and privacy rights. They argued that the Act's broad surveillance powers allowed the government to collect and analyze vast amounts of personal data, including phone records, internet activities, and financial transactions, without sufficient oversight or probable cause. These critics contended that such intrusive measures violated the Fourth Amendment's protection against unreasonable searches and seizures, and undermined the fundamental principles of a free and democratic society.

Furthermore, opponents of the Act questioned its effectiveness in preventing terrorism, pointing to instances of abuse and the lack of tangible evidence that the Act had significantly contributed to thwarting terrorist plots. They argued that the Act's provisions disproportionately targeted specific communities, leading to racial and religious profiling, and fostering a climate of fear and suspicion.

The debate also centered around the need for reform to strike a balance between security and civil liberties. Some argued for stricter oversight and increased transparency to ensure accountability, while others advocated for the modification or removal of certain provisions that were deemed overly intrusive or unconstitutional.

Ultimately, the debate surrounding the renewal and reform of the USA PATRIOT Act highlighted the complex trade-offs between national security and individual rights. It brought to the forefront questions regarding the appropriate limits of government surveillance and the need for effective counterterrorism measures that respect civil liberties. The outcome of this debate would have far-reaching implications on the protection of individual privacy and the preservation of democratic values in the United States.

Implications for democracy and citizen engagement

The USA PATRIOT Act, passed in the aftermath of the 9/11 terrorist attacks, has had far-reaching implications for democracy and citizen engagement in the United States. This subchapter explores the various ways in which the Act has impacted civil liberties, with a particular focus on its effects on individual rights and privacy.

One of the most significant implications of the USA PATRIOT Act is its potential to erode the principles of democracy. The Act grants sweeping surveillance powers to government agencies, such as the National Security Agency (NSA) and the Federal Bureau of Investigation (FBI), allowing them to monitor and collect information on individuals without sufficient oversight. This unchecked surveillance threatens the right to privacy, a fundamental component of democracy that ensures citizens can freely express themselves without fear of government intrusion.

Moreover, the Act has implications for citizen engagement by undermining trust in government institutions. The extensive surveillance powers granted by the Act have been seen by many as an infringement on the rights and freedoms of Americans. This has led to a climate of suspicion and skepticism, with citizens questioning the motives and actions of their government. Such erosion of trust can have serious consequences for citizen engagement, as individuals may be discouraged from participating in civic activities or exercising their democratic rights out of fear of being targeted or surveilled.

The USA PATRIOT Act also has implications for the balance of power between the government and its citizens. The Act grants law enforcement agencies broad powers to conduct searches and seizures in the name of national security, often without the need for a warrant. This can lead to the abuse of power, with innocent individuals being subjected to intrusive searches and seizures without proper justification. Such abuses can undermine the principle of due process, a cornerstone of democracy that ensures fair treatment and protection of individual rights.

Additionally, the Act has implications for the role of technology in democracy. The increased surveillance powers granted by the Act have been enabled by advancements in technology, such as the ability to collect and analyze vast amounts of data. This raises important questions about the ethical use of technology in democratic societies. As technology continues to evolve, policymakers, academics, and citizens must grapple with the implications of these advancements on civil liberties and citizen engagement.

In conclusion, the USA PATRIOT Act has had profound implications for democracy and citizen engagement in the United States. The Act's expansive surveillance powers, erosion of trust, and potential for abuse of power have all had a significant impact on individual rights and privacy. As we continue to analyze the effects of the Act, it is crucial to consider the long-term implications for democracy and citizen engagement in order to safeguard the principles and values that underpin our democratic society.

Chapter 11: International Perspectives on the USA PATRIOT Act

Examination of the Act's impact on global perceptions of the United States

The USA PATRIOT Act, enacted shortly after the 9/11 attacks, has had a significant impact not only on the civil liberties of American citizens but also on the global perceptions of the United States. This subchapter aims to delve into the Act's consequences on how the world views the United States and its commitment to human rights and individual freedoms.

The Act has garnered both praise and criticism from various countries, organizations, and individuals around the world. On one hand, some argue that the Act demonstrates the United States' determination to protect its citizens from potential terrorist threats. It is seen as a necessary measure in an era of heightened security concerns, and it has even influenced other nations to adopt similar legislation to combat terrorism within their own borders.

However, the Act has also faced vehement condemnation for its perceived infringement on civil liberties and privacy rights. Critics argue that the Act has eroded the United States' global reputation as a champion of human rights and individual freedoms. The expansion of surveillance powers, the broadening of government authority to access personal information, and the weakening of judicial oversight have raised concerns about unchecked government power and potential abuses.

These concerns have been amplified by the global reach of the Act. The Act's provisions extend beyond U.S. borders, allowing the government to access information held by foreign entities and even detain foreign nationals suspected of terrorist activities without due process. Such extraterritorial application of the Act has sparked widespread criticism and strained diplomatic relations with other countries.

The impact on global perceptions of the United States cannot be understated. The Act has created a perception that the United States is sacrificing civil liberties and privacy rights in the name of national security. This perception has had repercussions on international cooperation, information sharing, and trust in U.S. policies. It has also fueled anti-American sentiments and provided ammunition for critics of U.S. foreign policy.

Understanding the Act's impact on global perceptions is crucial for policymakers, government officials, and diplomats. It highlights the need for a delicate balance between security and civil liberties, as well as the importance of engaging in dialogue with the international community to address concerns and rebuild trust. By examining the Act's influence on global perceptions, we can gain valuable insights into the challenges faced by the United States in striking this balance and shaping a more secure and rights-respecting world.

Comparative analysis of counterterrorism measures in other countries

In the subchapter titled "Comparative analysis of counterterrorism measures in other countries," we delve into an exploration of how various nations have responded to the global threat of terrorism. By examining the counterterrorism strategies implemented by different countries, we aim to provide a comprehensive understanding of the effectiveness, implications, and potential consequences of these measures.

This comparative analysis is crucial in shedding light on the impact of counterterrorism policies on civil liberties, particularly in the context of the USA PATRIOT Act. As undergraduate and graduate students, high school students, academics and researchers, policy makers and government officials, journalists, business professionals, military and defense personnel, think tanks and analysts, general public, librarians and educators, non-government organizations, diplomats and international workers, and book club members, you will gain valuable insights into the global landscape of counterterrorism efforts.

We begin by examining the United Kingdom's response to terrorism, which includes legislation such as the Terrorism Act 2000 and the Counter-Terrorism and Security Act 2015. These laws have granted British authorities powers to detain and surveil suspects, raising concerns about the erosion of civil liberties.

Moving on to France, we explore the country's approach to counterterrorism, notably through the establishment of state of emergency legislation, which was implemented following the November 2015 Paris attacks. We analyze the implications of such measures, focusing on the balance between security and individual rights.

Germany's counterterrorism policies also warrant attention, particularly the Act on the Reform of the Constitution Protection and the German Intelligence Services, enacted in response to the rise of domestic extremism. We critically assess the impact of these measures on privacy and civil liberties.

Additionally, we explore the counterterrorism efforts of countries such as Australia, Canada, and Israel, each with their unique approaches to addressing the threat of terrorism. By analyzing their counterterrorism measures, we gain a broader perspective on the challenges faced by nations worldwide in striking a balance between security and civil liberties.

Throughout this subchapter, we emphasize the importance of understanding the global context of counterterrorism measures to fully comprehend the implications of the USA PATRIOT Act. By examining the experiences of other countries, we can critically evaluate the impact of the Act on individual rights and privacy, enabling us to engage in informed discussions, make informed policy decisions, and advocate for the protection of civil liberties in the fight against terrorism.

International human rights implications and diplomatic challenges

The USA PATRIOT Act, while enacted with the intention of enhancing national security, has raised serious concerns regarding its impact on civil liberties, both domestically and internationally. This subchapter aims to delve into the international human rights implications of the Act, as well as the diplomatic challenges it poses.

One of the key international human rights implications of the USA PATRIOT Act is the potential infringement on individual rights and privacy. The Act grants the government extensive powers to conduct surveillance, monitor communications, and access personal information without the need for a warrant. This has raised concerns about the erosion of privacy rights, as well as the potential for abuse of power.

Furthermore, the Act has faced criticism for its impact on freedom of expression and freedom of association. The broad definition of "domestic terrorism" under the Act has led to increased scrutiny and surveillance of individuals and groups engaged in political activism or dissent. This has had a chilling effect on the exercise of these fundamental rights, both domestically and internationally.

From a diplomatic perspective, the USA PATRIOT Act has created challenges in terms of international cooperation and trust. The Act enables the US government to obtain information from foreign governments and organizations, often without their knowledge or consent. This has strained relationships with allies and raised concerns about the protection of privacy and due process rights of individuals outside of the United States.

Moreover, the extraterritorial reach of the Act has raised questions about its compatibility with international law and the sovereignty of other nations. The Act grants the US government the authority to conduct surveillance and gather intelligence in foreign territories, potentially violating the rights and sovereignty of other nations.

These international human rights implications and diplomatic challenges demand careful consideration and evaluation. It is crucial for policymakers, government officials, and international workers to engage in dialogue and collaboration to address these concerns. International human rights standards should be upheld and respected, ensuring that any measures taken to enhance national security do not come at the expense of individual rights and privacy.

In conclusion, the USA PATRIOT Act's impact on civil liberties has significant international human rights implications and diplomatic challenges. It is vital for a wide range of audiences, including students, academics, policymakers, journalists, and the general public, to understand and critically analyze these implications to foster informed discussions and advocate for the protection of civil liberties.

Chapter 12: Future of Civil Liberties in the United States

Assessment of the long-term effects of the USA PATRIOT Act

Introduction:

The USA PATRIOT Act, enacted shortly after the tragic events of September 11, 2001, aimed to enhance national security and prevent terrorist activities within the United States. However, its impact on civil liberties has been a subject of concern and debate. This subchapter delves into the long-term effects of the USA PATRIOT Act, specifically examining its impact on individual rights and privacy.

1. Erosion of Privacy:

One of the primary concerns surrounding the USA PATRIOT Act is its potential infringement on privacy. The Act grants law enforcement agencies broad surveillance powers, including the ability to access personal information, monitor communications, and conduct searches without obtaining a warrant. This erosion of privacy has raised concerns about the extent to which government agencies can intrude into the lives of individuals, potentially violating their constitutional rights.

2. Expansion of Government Surveillance:

The USA PATRIOT Act has significantly expanded the scope of government surveillance, particularly through provisions such as the collection of business records and the use of National Security Letters (NSLs). These powers have enabled law enforcement agencies to obtain sensitive information about individuals, including financial records, medical history, and internet browsing habits. The long-term effect is the creation of a surveillance state, where individuals may feel constantly monitored, leading to self-censorship and a chilling effect on free speech.

3. Impact on Minority Communities:

The USA PATRIOT Act has had a disproportionately negative impact on minority communities. The Act has been criticized for enabling racial and ethnic profiling, leading to increased surveillance and discrimination against Muslim, Arab, and South Asian communities. The long-term consequences include a loss of trust between these communities and law enforcement agencies, as well as a potential chilling effect on their participation in civic activities.

4. Judicial Oversight and Accountability:

Another aspect worth assessing is the level of judicial oversight and accountability over the implementation of the USA PATRIOT Act. Critics argue that the Act has weakened the traditional checks and balances system, granting excessive power to the executive branch. This lack of oversight has raised concerns about potential abuses and violations of civil liberties, prompting calls for greater transparency and accountability in the long-term.

Conclusion:

The long-term effects of the USA PATRIOT Act on civil liberties have been significant and continue to shape the landscape of individual rights and privacy in the United States. The erosion of privacy, expansion of government surveillance, impact on minority communities, and questions of judicial oversight and accountability all warrant further examination and discussion. By critically analyzing these effects, policymakers, researchers, and the general public can better understand the implications of the Act and work towards finding a balance between national security and the protection of civil liberties.

Predictions for the future of civil liberties in the United States

As we examine the impact of the USA PATRIOT Act on civil liberties, it is crucial to consider the future trajectory of individual rights and privacy in the United States. The implications of this legislation have far-reaching consequences that will shape the landscape of civil liberties for years to come. In this subchapter, we will explore several predictions for the future of civil liberties in the United States.

1. Enhanced Surveillance and Privacy Concerns: The USA PATRIOT Act has significantly expanded the government's surveillance powers, allowing for increased monitoring of citizens' activities. As technology continues to evolve, we anticipate that surveillance capabilities will become even more sophisticated, raising concerns about privacy infringement and the potential abuse of power by government agencies.

2. Legal Challenges and Judicial Scrutiny: Given the contentious nature of the USA PATRIOT Act, it is likely that legal challenges will emerge in the future. These challenges will question the constitutionality of various provisions, leading to judicial scrutiny and potential revisions to the legislation. The outcome of these legal battles will have profound implications for civil liberties.

3. Balancing National Security and Individual Rights: The tension between national security and individual rights will persist in the future. As threats evolve, policymakers will face the ongoing challenge of striking a balance between protecting citizens and preserving civil liberties. This delicate equilibrium will require constant reassessment and public discourse.

4. Legislative Reforms: Over time, there will likely be calls for legislative reforms to address the concerns raised by the USA PATRIOT Act. These reforms may aim to narrow the scope of surveillance powers, increase transparency and accountability, and strengthen privacy protections. The effectiveness of such reforms will depend on the political climate and public demand for change.

5. Technological Advancements and New Challenges: Rapid advancements in technology will present new challenges to civil liberties in the future. Emerging technologies such as artificial intelligence, facial recognition, and biometric data collection will require robust legal frameworks to ensure that individual rights are protected in the digital age.

6. Public Awareness and Activism: As the public becomes increasingly aware of the implications of the USA PATRIOT Act and other legislation impacting civil liberties, we anticipate a rise in activism and advocacy for privacy rights. This grassroots movement will play a crucial role in shaping the future of civil liberties, mobilizing public opinion, and driving legislative change.

In conclusion, the future of civil liberties in the United States is uncertain and contingent upon various factors such as technological advancements, legal challenges, and public awareness. The impact of the USA PATRIOT Act will continue to shape the trajectory of civil liberties, necessitating ongoing scrutiny, dialogue, and action to safeguard individual rights and privacy in the digital age.

Recommendations for safeguarding civil liberties while addressing security concerns

Introduction:

As the USA PATRIOT Act continues to shape the landscape of national security and civil liberties, it is crucial to strike a balance between safeguarding individual rights and addressing security concerns. This subchapter aims to provide recommendations for policymakers, government officials, and all concerned stakeholders to ensure the protection of civil liberties while effectively addressing security challenges.

1. Enhancing Judicial Oversight:

One of the key recommendations is to strengthen judicial oversight and accountability. This can be achieved by establishing an independent panel of judges who can provide oversight for surveillance activities, ensuring that they are conducted in accordance with the law and not infringing on civil liberties.

2. Safeguarding Privacy:

To protect individual privacy, it is important to establish clear guidelines for data collection and retention by intelligence agencies. Policies should be enacted to limit the collection, use, and retention of personal information to what is strictly necessary for national security purposes. Regular audits should be conducted to ensure compliance with these guidelines.

3. Transparency and Reporting:

To maintain public trust, there should be increased transparency in the activities of intelligence agencies. Regular reports should be published, outlining the number and nature of surveillance activities conducted, as well as the number of individuals affected. This will allow for public scrutiny and enable informed debates on the balance between security and civil liberties.

4. Minimization of Overreach:

Efforts should be made to minimize overreach in surveillance activities. This can be achieved by adopting a targeted approach to intelligence gathering, focusing on individuals or groups suspected of involvement in criminal or terrorist activities, rather than broad-based surveillance of the general population. This will help prevent the infringement of civil liberties while still addressing security concerns effectively.

5. Strengthening Whistleblower Protections:

To ensure accountability and prevent abuse of power, robust whistleblower protections should be put in place. Individuals who come forward with evidence of misconduct or violations of civil liberties should be protected from retaliation and provided with legal avenues to report such abuses.

Conclusion:

In conclusion, safeguarding civil liberties while addressing security concerns is a complex task that requires a careful balance. The recommendations provided above aim to ensure that individual rights are protected while still allowing for effective national security measures. By implementing these recommendations, policymakers and other concerned stakeholders can work towards a society that upholds civil liberties while effectively addressing security challenges.

Conclusion: Reflections and Key Takeaways

Summary of the book's main findings and arguments

In "Unveiling the USA PATRIOT Act: Analyzing its Impact on Civil Liberties," the author delves into the effects of the USA PATRIOT Act on individual rights and privacy. This subchapter aims to provide a concise summary of the book's main findings and arguments.

The book begins by outlining the historical context that led to the passing of the USA PATRIOT Act in the aftermath of the September 11, 2001 terrorist attacks. It highlights the perceived need for enhanced security measures to prevent future attacks and the political climate that facilitated the Act's swift passage.

The main finding of the book is that while the USA PATRIOT Act was indeed instrumental in bolstering national security efforts, it has had significant implications for civil liberties. The Act granted law enforcement agencies expanded surveillance powers, including the ability to access personal records, monitor communications, and conduct searches without probable cause.

One of the key arguments put forth by the author is that the USA PATRIOT Act has led to a erosion of privacy rights. The Act's provisions have allowed for the collection of vast amounts of personal data, raising concerns about government overreach and potential abuse of power. The book presents evidence of instances where innocent individuals have been subject to unwarranted surveillance, leading to a chilling effect on free speech and expression.

Another important argument made in the book is that the USA PATRIOT Act has disproportionately impacted marginalized communities. The Act's broad definitions and vague language have resulted in increased profiling and targeting of individuals based on race, ethnicity, religion, and political beliefs. This has perpetuated systemic biases and contributed to instances of discrimination and surveillance of innocent individuals.

Furthermore, the book highlights the need for a balance between security measures and safeguarding civil liberties. It argues that while national security is of utmost importance, it should not come at the expense of individual rights and privacy. The author suggests that greater oversight, transparency, and accountability mechanisms should be put in place to mitigate the potential abuses of the Act.

Overall, "Unveiling the USA PATRIOT Act: Analyzing its Impact on Civil Liberties" provides a comprehensive examination of the Act's consequences on individual rights and privacy. It serves as a critical resource for undergraduate and graduate students, policymakers, journalists, and the general public interested in understanding the complex relationship between security and civil liberties in the post-9/11 era.

Importance of ongoing discourse and examination of civil liberties

Subchapter: Importance of ongoing discourse and examination of civil liberties

Introduction:

In the wake of the USA PATRIOT Act, it has become imperative for individuals from all walks of life to engage in continuous discourse and examination of civil liberties. This subchapter delves into the significance of ongoing discussions surrounding civil liberties and emphasizes the need for constant scrutiny to safeguard individual rights and privacy. By exploring the impact of the USA PATRIOT Act on civil liberties, we aim to foster a deeper understanding of the consequences of such legislation.

Importance of Ongoing Discourse:

Ongoing discourse serves as a vital tool in ensuring the preservation of civil liberties. By engaging in continuous discussions, undergraduate and graduate students, high school students, academics, researchers, and policy makers can collectively evaluate the implications of the USA PATRIOT Act on individual rights and privacy. This discourse enables us to identify potential abuses of power and develop strategies to mitigate them, ensuring the protection of civil liberties.

Examination of Civil Liberties:

Thorough examination of civil liberties is crucial to understanding the full impact of the USA PATRIOT Act. Journalists, business professionals, military and defense personnel, think tanks, analysts, and the general public must actively assess the effects of this legislation on personal freedoms and privacy rights. By examining civil liberties, we can shed light on any potential infringements and advocate for necessary amendments to strike a balance between national security and individual rights.

Role of Librarians and Educators:

Librarians and educators play a pivotal role in disseminating knowledge and facilitating discussions on civil liberties. They can provide resources, organize workshops, and encourage critical thinking among students and the wider community. By empowering individuals with information, librarians and educators facilitate the ongoing discourse necessary to safeguard civil liberties.

Engaging Non-Government Organizations and Diplomats:

Non-government organizations, diplomats, and international workers bring unique perspectives to the discourse on civil liberties. Their experiences in different socio-political contexts contribute to a more comprehensive understanding of the impact of the USA PATRIOT Act on individual rights and privacy. By actively engaging these stakeholders, we can develop a global perspective that transcends national boundaries.

Conclusion:

In conclusion, ongoing discourse and examination of civil liberties are of paramount importance in understanding the consequences of the USA PATRIOT Act on individual rights and privacy. By involving undergraduate and graduate students, high school students, academics and researchers, policy makers and government officials, journalists, business professionals, military and defense personnel, think tanks and analysts, the general public, librarians and educators, non-government organizations, diplomats and international workers, and book clubs in this discourse, we can collectively work towards striking a balance between national security and individual freedoms. Only through continuous scrutiny can we ensure the protection of civil liberties in an ever-changing landscape.

Final thoughts on the balance between security and individual rights

As we conclude our exploration of the USA PATRIOT Act and its impact on civil liberties, it is crucial to reflect on the delicate balance between security and individual rights that this legislation seeks to achieve. Throughout this book, we have examined the far-reaching consequences of the Act on various aspects of our lives, particularly on individual rights and privacy. Now, it is time to ponder and evaluate the implications of this balance.

The USA PATRIOT Act was enacted in response to the devastating terrorist attacks on September 11, 2001. Its primary objective was to enhance national security and protect American citizens from future acts of terrorism. However, in pursuing this objective, the Act has raised concerns about potential infringements on civil liberties.

On one hand, the Act has undoubtedly bolstered the government's ability to prevent terrorist activities. It has provided law enforcement agencies with necessary tools to investigate and prosecute terrorism-related crimes. The Act has facilitated information sharing between intelligence agencies, improved surveillance capabilities, and strengthened border security. These measures have undoubtedly contributed to safeguarding the nation and its citizens.

On the other hand, critics argue that the Act has encroached upon individual rights and privacy. The expanded surveillance powers granted to law enforcement agencies have raised concerns about unwarranted intrusions into the lives of innocent citizens. The broad scope of surveillance, encompassing electronic communications, financial transactions, and library records, has stirred fears of government overreach and a chilling effect on free speech.

Finding the right equilibrium between security and individual rights is an ongoing challenge. While the USA PATRIOT Act has undoubtedly enhanced security, it is crucial to continually reassess its provisions to ensure the preservation of civil liberties. Striking a balance requires robust oversight mechanisms, judicial review, and transparency in implementing the Act's provisions.

It is imperative for policymakers, government officials, and citizens alike to engage in informed discussions about the impact of the USA PATRIOT Act on civil liberties. Academics, researchers, and think tanks play a vital role in conducting rigorous research and analysis to shed light on the Act's consequences. Journalists must continue to hold those in power accountable, ensuring transparency and public discourse.

Ultimately, the final judgment on the balance between security and individual rights lies in the hands of the American people. Every citizen must actively participate in shaping the policies and laws that govern our nation, ensuring that both security and individual rights remain protected. It is through these collective efforts that we can strive for a society that upholds the fundamental principles of democracy while effectively combating terrorism.

www.ingramcontent.com/pod-product-compliance
Lightning Source LLC
Chambersburg PA
CBHW051302160726
47994CB00003B/1277